THE AŚVAMEDHA

THE AŚVAMEDHA

The Rite and its Logic

SUBHASH KAK

MOTILAL BANARSIDASS PUBLISHERS
PRIVATE LIMITED • DELHI

First Edition: *Delhi, 2002*
Reprint: *Delhi, 2004*

ISBN: 81-208-1877-6

MOTILAL BANARSIDASS
41 U.A. Bungalow Road, Jawahar Nagar, Delhi 110 007
8 Mahalaxmi Chamber, 22 Bhulabhai Desai Road, Mumbai 400 026
236, 9th Main III Block, Jayanagar, Bangalore 560 011
120 Royapettah High Road, Mylapore, Chennai 600 004
Sanas Plaza, 1302 Baji Rao Road, Pune 411 002
8 Camac Street, Kolkata 700 017
Ashok Rajpath, Patna 800 004
Chowk, Varanasi 221 001

Printed in India
BY JAINENDRA PRAKASH JAIN AT SHRI JAINENDRA PRESS,
A-45 NARAINA, PHASE-I, NEW DELHI 110 028
AND PUBLISHED BY SUNDARLAL JAIN FOR
MOTILAL BANARSIDASS, BUNGALOW ROAD, DELHI 110 007

Contents

Preface

The Aśvamedha sacrifice has been a subject of great fascination in India and elsewhere. It is described as one of the most significant rituals in the Indian texts, and Western authors have been much intrigued by the scale of the rite and its drama.

The horse in Indian mythology stands for the Sun. The sea is taken to be its stable and its birthplace. This reference is to the primal "waters" surrounding the earth from which the Sun emerges everyday. Other nations also took the horse to be a symbol for the Sun. The Chinese, the Greeks, the Romans, and the Russians saw a link between the horse and the sea. This idea was transferred in popular mythology to the vast Equine-head in the sea. The fire issuing from its mouth is the Vaḍavānala, which is the fire of the Sun hidden in Canopus in the southern celestial hemisphere. The Aśvamedha is the sacrifice of the annual renewal of the Sun at the New Year and that of the accompanying renewal of the king's rule. At the spiritual level, it is a celebration to get reconnected to the inner Sun.

A few months ago, my friend Vish Murthy wrote me asking me to write on the nature and logic of this rite. This brief essay is a response to that request. I am thankful to several friends and colleagues, in particular Narahari Achar, Bhadraiah Mallampalli, and Lalita Pandit, who gave me valuable comments on earlier versions of the manuscript.

Baton Rouge, Śivarātri
February 21, 2001

SUBHASH KAK

1

Introduction

This essay describes several aspects of the Aśvamedha rite, the "horse-sacrifice," and summarizes its logic. This rite is a great state function in which ritual elements are woven together with secular ceremonies to make an assertion of monarchical authority. It is called the king of sacrifice in the Śatapatha Brāhmaṇa (SB 13.2.2.1), whose Kāṇḍa 13 is devoted exclusively to the rite.

Before we proceed, we emphasize that the use of the word "sacrifice," with its common meaning of "killing to offer to God or gods," is cause of much misunderstanding of the Vedic ritual. Vedic yajña (sacrifice) need not involve any killing of animals. It is a highly symbolic performance, and the animals of the sacrifice may be clay images or grains; or they may just be specific utterances. The Chāndogya Upaniṣad, speaking of Revatī Sāmans says, "The hiṅkāra is goats, the prastāva sheep, the udgītha cows, the pratihāra horses, and the nidhana puruṣa" (CU 2.6.1; 2.18.1).

When an animal is sacrificed in the ritual, we are speaking of mock killing in sacred theatre. The word "killing" is described in the texts to apply equally to the pressing of the soma stalks and the grinding of the grain (TS 6.6.9.2, SB 2.2.2.1-2, 4.3.4.1-2, 11.1.2.1). This is not to say that "animal" sacrifice has never been taken literally in India, but we will show that the normative meaning of the term is symbolic.

With this special meaning of the word "sacrifice" in mind, we note that a large number of animals are sacrificed in the Aśvamedha rite. Chapters 22-25 of the Vājasaneyi Saṃhitā constitute the mantras to be read at the rite; the Taittirīya Saṃhitā has considerable material on it, scattered in several sections. This rite is not emphasized by all early books. The Aitareya and Kauṣītaki Brāhmaṇas have nothing on it. The Ṛgveda 1.162 and 1.163 describe the sacrificial horse. The rite, as described in RV 1.162, appears to involve only two animals, the goat (aja) and the horse (vāji, aśva). But note that SB 7.5.2.21 says *vāk vā'ajaḥ*, aja is speech. Also, SB 9.2.3.40 says *tad yad dadhidrapsa 'upatiṣthate tadeva paśurūpam*, the drop of yoghurt is a form of the animal; and SB 9.2.3.46 says *asthīni vai samidhḥ, māṃsāni vā 'āhutayaḥ*, the logs are the bones, and the oblations (of ghee) are the flesh. So the flesh of the horse and the flies on it mentioned in RV 1.162.9 appear to be the ghee and the flies on it. TS 2.3.2.8 says *dadhi madhu ghṛtamāpo dhānā bhavantyetadvai paśūnāṃ rūpam*, yoghurt, honey, ghee, water, and grain are certainly the forms of (the five) animals. Dayānanda Sarasvatī and his followers take RV 1.162 to be a hymn on the heroic sacrificial horse who is being tended to by attendants.

The Vedic view acknowledges that all creation is interdependent. It is asserted that *ayam ātmā brahma*, the Ātman contains the entire universe. Likewise, the body has within it all creatures. Of the principal animals conceived within the body, the horse represents time. The horse-sacrifice is then the most mystical and powerful, because it touches upon the mystery of time, which carries within it the secret of immortality.

The sacrifice of the animals is the enactment of the killing of the mortal lower self for a transformation into the immortal higher self. Since the higher self cannot manifest itself without the lower one, one must settle for something less, a ritual rebirth of the individual. In other words, sacrifice deals with mastery of time.

From here, the next step is the cause of time, or the Sun. The Ṛgveda (1.163.2) says that the horse is symbolic of the Sun. In VS 11.12 it is said of the horse, "In heaven is your highest birth, in air your navel, on earth your home." Here the horse is being symbolized by the sacrificial fire. SB 13.3.3.3 says that Aśvamedha is the Sun, while SB 11.2.5.4

says that it is to be done year after year. Aśva also means the horse, so it is the horse sacrifice for the courser in the skies.

This is how the Taittirīya Saṃhitā describes the sacrificial horse of the Aśvamedha:

> The head of the sacrificial horse is the dawn, the eye the Sun, the breath the wind, the ear the Moon, the feet the quarters, the ribs the intermediate quarters, the winking the day and night, the joints the half-months, the joinings the months, the limbs the seasons, the trunk the year, the hair the rays (of the Sun), the form the Nakṣatra, the bones the stars, the flesh the mist, the hair the plants, the tail hairs the tress, the mouth Agni, the open (mouth) Vaiśvānara, the belly the sea, the anus the atmosphere, the testicles the sky and the earth, the *membrum virile* the pressing-stone, the seed the soma. (TS 7.5.25)

In other words, the whole universe is the sacrificial horse. An actual horse represented the "sacrificial" horse in part of the ritual; elsewhere the representation was by other objects.

It may be that aśva was a primary name for the Sun that was later applied to the horse. The celestial horse was supposed to spring from the sea (cosmic waters enveloping the earth) and return to it. The Purāṇas use the image of a fire-breathing mare that lives in the sea. As an Equine-head, it is called Vadavāmukha and the fire coming out of its mouth is called Vadavānala. It is a visualization of what happens to the Sun as it sinks in the primal waters.

This rite has been commented on by several scholars.[1] But this examination has been mainly regarding the details of the rite in the Śatapatha and its descriptions in later Sanskrit literature, such as the Mahābhārata and the Rāmāyaṇa. The Indian medieval commentators such as Uvaṭa, Mahīdhara, and Bhaṭṭa Bhāskara take the ritual literally. But their views do not completely square with the earliest accounts in the Śatapatha and the Ṛgveda. It appears that the medieval ritualists were projecting their contemporary attitudes in their embellishments of the narrative.

The Mahābhārata account of the rite is quite fragmentary. Although the 14th Parvan of the epic is devoted to the performance of the Aśvamedha yajña by Yudhiṣṭhira, very little is written on the rite itself. It is stated that the rite will take place on the full Moon of the month of Caitra. A mention of twenty-one stakes is made, as of the piling of a falcon Agnicayana altar.[2]Likewise, the Rāmāyaṇa also glosses over the ritual in just a few verses.

Horses and Cattle

For some time the analysis of the Aśvamedha rite got entangled with the 19th century race-based theories about conquest of India by cattle-driving outsiders whose use of the horse gave them military superiority. It was believed that the importance of the horse in the ritual arose out of this military use. But recent archaeological findings have shown no evidence of any racial conflict or mass-migrations.

Horses have roamed the earth for millions of years. The genus Equus appeared in early Pliocene of Northern America; around 2.5 million years ago it dispersed to Asia (*E. sanmeniensis, E. sivalensis, E. namadicus*), Europe (*E. stenonis, E. livenzovensis*) and then Africa (*E. koobiforensis*). A later movement brought *E. hemionus* and *E. caballus* to Eurasia. Equus also dispersed in the middle and late Pleistocene into Southern America. With the exception of Australia and Antarctica, it had a worldwide distribution and survived undisturbed until about 10,000 years ago, when overhunting by prehistoric man brought it to a drastic reduction in Eurasia, and to extinction in the Americas, where it was reintroduced in post-Columbian times.

In the Old World, horses are depicted in cave paintings in France that are up to 20,000 years old. Analysis of horse teeth suggests that riding began about 6,000 years ago.[3]While the Indian horse *E. sivalensis* is supposed to have become extinct about 50,000 years ago, other sub-species emerged that have the general features of the horse described in the Vedic books. The Vedic horse has 34 ribs, against the 36 ribs of the Central Asian horse.

Genetic studies of Indian cattle has shown that it is a distinct sub-species that separated from the Middle Eastern and the European cattle, tens of thousands of years ago. Cattle remains have been found that go back to the earliest level of the Indic tradition in Mehrgarh that has been dated to 6500 BC. The new evidence on the distinctiveness of the Indian horse and the cattle establishes that the military function could have played no role in the choice of the horse in the ritual.

Paradox, Transcendence

There have been several modern scholarly studies of the concept of sacrifice. According to one view, sacrifice is just an invention of scholars.[4] This is, of course, not true. According to another, sacrifice provides a means to the community to redirect feelings of violence and aggression, saving it from collapse.[5] Sacrifice is then a social construct of great use, and it has elements of competition and gift-giving woven into it. The victim is both outcast and saviour, and being separate from others, the king is often the ideal (but not real) victim. This may explain elements of sacrifice in many societies, but sacrifice is not a unitary experience. There are many varieties of it which will fall outside any theory, and the Vedic sacrifice is one of them.

The distinctiveness of Vedic sacrifice comes from many reasons of which the following two are the main ones: (i) Its ambiguities are much deeper than sacrifice elsewhere, and it operates at several levels, including the spiritual; and more uniquely, (ii) it posits an identity of the Sacrificer and the universe. This latter idea is perhaps why the "knowledge" central to the sacrifice becomes, in the end, the purpose of the sacrifice. This knowledge becomes the vehicle of the transformation of the participants. The "theatre" aspect of the ritual is, therefore, considerably accentuated.

Given this background, it is not surprising to see Heesterman, a scholar of Vedic sacrifice, summarize:[6] "Sacrifice can perhaps be best seen as a 'play' that makes the tensions and uncertainties visible by breaking them down into separate well-defined acts and throwing their ambiguity into relief. In this way it turns tension into conflict, ambivalence into paradox, uncertainty into impending disaster, and disaster into triumph."

Heesterman is essentially paraphrasing what the Vedic ritualists themselves say about sacrifice. But, he is less perceptive when he sees the Vedic sacrifice emerge out of a mythology of fire:[7] "[S]ince man's appropriation of the fire, its care and exploitation had been an inexhaustible source of creative imagination and ratiocinative reflection. Made and cultivated by man the fire—*his* fire—was directly related to him in an ambivalent and tensely personal way... While in ancient Iran the fire, enthroned in its temple, was made to transcend self and community, the Vedic ritualists went the opposite way. They maximized the personal bond of man and his fire. The fire and its cult were drawn into man's individual self, the *ātman*. Not the ambivalent and unpredictable fire but the *ātman* was to encompass and control life and death. As such it could not but be the seat of immortality. In other words, the individual self, the *ātman*, was made to transcend both fire and community."

The idea of the abstract sacrifice is already the centerstage of the Ṛgvedic hymns, so to see a development from the physical to the spiritual beyond the Ṛgveda is wrong. But there is more than just the idea of sacrifice in this text. Antonio de Nicolas is correct when he says that to see the Ṛgveda as a book of rituals, a religio-cultural mythology, or an esoteric spiritual document is merely to scratch its surface structure. He argues that one must take it as a linguistic whole, with four languages of:

1. Non-existence (*asat*)

2. Existence (*sat*)

3. Images and Sacrifice (*yajña*)

4. Embodied (*ṛta*) vision (*dhīḥ*).

He adds,[8] "These four languages function as four spaces of discourse, four ways of viewing the world within which human action takes place and from which any statement in the text gains meaning. The languages of Non-existence, Existence, Images and Sacrifice show the human situation within certain disparate linguistic contexts embodying different ways of viewing the world... A *complementarity* of languages is suggested under a transcendent and unifying language: and each language is torn from its opposing demands of exclusivity in exchange for a way of viewing and acting in the world which is eternally (*nitya*) efficient."

The different languages of the Ṛgveda address the four different aspects of our reality: (i) physical existence, (ii) mind, consciousness, spirit, (iii) transformation, and (iv) embodied vision. The languages of asat and sat also relate to the present and its creative renewal. These four aspects are interdependent, so the languages required to describe them are context-sensitive.

Like the Ṛgveda, Vedic sacrifice operates through several languages. Behind the drama of the actual performance are several narratives regarding non-existence, existence, change, and embodied vision. The performance picks up elements of these narratives as it goes along, rendering the performance esoteric and paradoxical.

This essay describes the Aśvamedha rite and its symbolism. This is used to explain distinctive aspects of the Vedic sacrifice system. Several questions related to the Aśvamedha are posed and answered in the context of Vedic epistemology.

The Aśvamedha rite has several functions: (i) It presents an equivalence of the nākṣatra year to the heaven, implying that it is a rite that celebrates the rebirth of the Sun; (ii) it is symbolic of the conquest of Time by the king, in whose name the rite is performed; (iii) it is a celebration of social harmony achieved by the transcendence of the fundamental conflicts between various sources of power. Numbers from another Vedic rite, the Agnicayana, help in the understanding of several of its details.

2

Sacrifice, Sacred Theatre

The central idea behind the Vedic system is the notion of bandhu (bindings or connections) between the astronomical, the terrestrial, the physiological, and the spiritual. These connections are described in terms of number of characteristics, such as the 360 bones of the infant (which later fuse into the 206 bones of the adult) and the 360 days of the year. In a similar vein, the Garbha Upaniṣad says that the body has 180 sutures, 900 sinews. The Bṛhadāraṇyaka Upaniṣad takes the number of nāḍīs to be 72,000. All these numbers are related to 360, the nominal day count of the year.

One can see a plausible basis behind the equivalences. Modern research has shown that all life comes with its inner clocks. Living organisms have rhythms that are matched to the periods of the Sun or the Moon. There are quite precise biological clocks of 24-hour (according to the day), 24 hour 50 minutes (according to the lunar day since the Moon rises roughly 50 minutes later every day) or its half representing the tides, 29.5 days (the period from one new Moon to the next), and the year. Monthly rhythms, averaging 29.5 days, are reflected in the reproductive cycles of many marine plants and those of animals. The menstrual period is a synodic month and the average duration of pregnancy is nine synodic months. There are other biological periodicities of longer durations.

It is reasonable to assume that the Vedic thinkers were aware of these connections, as were the ancient people in other cultures. The uniqueness of the Vedic vision was the extension of the bindings to the body to those in the inner landscape of the spirit.

The Vedic rites were meant to help the participant transform themselves. This was accomplished through sacrifice. The rishis saw the universe as going through unceasing change in a cycle of birth and death, potentially free yet, paradoxically, governed by order. This order was reflected in the bandhu between the planets, the elements of the body, and the mind. At the deepest level, the whole universe was bound to, and reflected in, the individual consciousness, as proclaimed in the mahāvākyas *aham brahmāsmi* and *yat piṇḍe tad brahmāṇḍe*.

Vedic ritual is a highly systematized performance of various elements, that include manipulations, formulas, liturgy, exchanges, where some of these elements are varied according to the specific rite. These elements have symbolic significance. The basic pattern is that of the iṣṭi, the preparation or offering of one or more cakes or bowls of porridge.

There are three kinds of rites: *kāmya, nitya*, and *naimittika*. The *kāmya* rites are optional rites; the *nitya* rites are the compulsory, cyclic ones; the *naimittika* are the ones prescribed for specific occasion, and so they also occur with regularity. The Gopatha Brāhmaṇa gives the following order for the performance of the sacrifices: Āgnyādheya, Pūrṇāhuti, Agnihotra, Darśa-pūrṇa-māsa, Āgrayaṇa, Cāturmāsya, Paśubandha, Agniṣṭoma, Rājasūya, Aśvamedha, Puruṣamedha, and Sarvamedha (GB 5.7).

The place of sacrifice represents the cosmos. Three fires are used, which stand for the three divisions of space. The course of the sacrifice represents the year, and all such ritual forms part of continuing annual performances. The rite culminates in the ritual rebirth of the yajamāna, which signifies the regeneration of his universe. It is sacred theatre, built upon paradoxes of reality, where symbolic deaths of animals and humans, including the yajamāna himself, may be enacted.

The riddle of the sacrifice is best expressed in the *Asya Vāmasya* hymn (RV 1.164):

pṛcchāmi tvā param antam pṛthivyāḥ
pṛcchāmi yatra bhuvanasya nābhiḥ
pṛcchāmi tvā vṛṣṇo aśvasya retaḥ
pṛcchāmi vācaḥ paramaṃ vyoma

iyaṃ vediḥ paro antaḥ pṛthivyā
ayaṃ yajño bhuvanasya nābhiḥ
ayaṃ somo vṛṣṇo aśvasya reto
brahmāyaṃ vācaḥ paramaṃ vyoma

I ask you about the farthest end of the earth
I ask you about the navel of the universe
I ask you about the seed of the bursting horse
I ask you about the final abode of speech

This altar is the farthest end of the earth
This sacrifice is the navel of the universe
The soma is the seed of the bursting horse
This voice is the final abode of speech

The mystery of the sacrifice, with its suspension between life and death, reality and magic, logic and mystical experience is communicated in a language which is full of paradox. For example, it is stated that Prajāpati is Agni's father, but he is also Agni's son (SB 6.1.2.26); also, *yajñena yajñam ayajanta devas*, the gods sacrificed to the sacrifice with the sacrifice (RV 1.164.50).

The sacrifice is not the drama associated with it, but rather the transformation accruing from it. Says Kena Upaniṣad 2.3:

yasyāmataṃ tasya mataṃ mataṃ yasya na veda saḥ. avijñātaṃ vijānatāṃ vijñātamavijānatāṃ

He by whom Brahman is not known, knows it; he by whom it is known, knows it not. It is not

> known by those who know it; it is known by those who do not know it" (KeU 2.3)

Vedic ritual is also related to the ongoing struggle between the devas and the asuras, where the devas represent the higher cognitive centers in man, and the asuras represent the lower centers that are associated with the body.[9] Viewed as independent agents, the asuras are materialists, content with the identity of the body with their self; this is described aptly in the dialogue between Prajāpati, Virocana, and Indra (CU 8.7-14). The devas need to subdue the asuras to establish order. The asuras are older because the body comes first; the devas are the younger descendents of Prajāpati (BU 1.3.1).

The prototypical sacrifice is that of Vṛtra, who represents the covering that separates the individual self from the inner Sun (SB 1.1.3.4). Indra, as the deity of the atmosphere, must make this sacrifice. Indra kills Vṛtra by the offering of a cake (SB 5.2.3.7).

The horse appears in the Ṛgveda in connection with the story of Dadhyañc, the son of Atharvaṇa, who knows the mystery of sacrifice. Dadhyañc is the teacher of madhu-vidyā, the mystical doctrine that brahman is present everywhere (SB 4.1.5.18). The name of this vidyā comes from the essence of sweetness in all flowers, transformed by bees into honey, which is not apparent to everyone. Upon Dadhyañc a horse-head is placed by the Aśvins, who wish to learn his knowledge (RV 1.117.22). This story is explained in SB 14.1.1.18-24:

> Now, Dadhyañc Ātharvaṇa knew this essence, this sacrifice—how ths head of the sacrifice is put on again, how this sacrifice becomes complete. Indra said to him, "If you teach this (mystery) to anyone else, I will cut off your head."
>
> Now, the Aśvins heard this: "Dadhyañc Ātharvaṇa knows this pure essence, this sacrifice—how this head of the sacrifice is put on again, how this sacrifice becomes complete."

> They went to him and said, "Let us be your pupils." He asked, "What do you wish to learn?"
>
> "This pure essence, this sacrifice—how the head of sacrifice is put on again, how the sacrifice becomes complete," they replied.
>
> He said, "Indra has told me, 'If you teach it to anyone else, I will cut off your head.' Therefore, I fear that he might indeed cut off my head. I will not accept you as pupils."
>
> They said, "We two will protect you from him."
>
> "How will you protect me?" he asked.
>
> They said, "When you accept us as your pupils, we will cut off your head and put it aside elsewhere. Then we will bring the head of a horse and put it on you, and you will teach us with it. When you have taught us, Indra will cut off that head of yours. Then we will bring your own head, and put it on you again." He agreed and accepted them as pupils.
>
> When he had received them as pupils, they cut off his head and put it aside elsewhere, and having brought the head of a horse, they placed it on him. With that head he taught them. And when he had taught them, Indra cut off that head of his. Then they brought his own head and placed it on him again.

This story provides a lesson about the meaning of sacrifice. Dadhyañc Ātharvaṇa, SB 6.4.2.3 tells us, is speech, which is the true vehicle of sacrifice. Speech has the power to transform and it transforms the speaker himself. Having spoken, one is not the same person, so the sacrifice causes one to lose one's original head. The horse's head (here symbolizing time) is the source of this transcendent knowledge.

There is another reference to Dadhyañc in the Ṛgveda (1.84). Here Indra uses his bones to slay ninety-nine Vṛtras.

There are various versions of this story. In one, Indra finds the bones of a dead Dadhyañc to fashion a thunderbolt to slay the asurās. In the Mahābhārata 12.343 version of the story, Dadhyañc, upon hearing of the unstoppable power of the asura Viśvarūpa, the son of Tvaṣṭṛ, gives up his body so that Indra can fashion a thunderbolt out of his bones. With this irresistible weapon, Indra triumphs over Viśvarūpa. This shows how words, even old ones like the bones of Dadhyañc represent, have the power to vanquish ignorance.

Masks and Sandhyā-bhāṣā

Sacrifice is also performance. To understand Vedic ritual it is helpful to see how theatrical performance was enacted in the ancient world. In such performance, whether it took place in India, or Greece, Rome or elsewhere, masks were used to convey the sense of paradox and transformation.

The earliest Indian rock art, from the Mesolithic and the Neolithic eras that predate the Harappan civilization, has figures wearing masks.[10]Terracota masks have been found in Harappa; these include a goat mask. The much later Nāṭyaśāstra prescribes the use of mukharāga to paint different masks directly on the actor's face.[11]

Masks were used by actors for dramatic effect to convey danger, mystery, and to facilitate the sense of transformation in the viewer's mind. The actor could take the persona of gods, demons, or of animals. It also made it possible to show killing in symbolic terms, with great power.

The use of masks, so pervasive in the theatrical performances of Classical Greece and Rome, was suppressed by the medieval Church. In the words of David Napier:[12]

> [W]hat distinguished medieval visual representations was the conviction that all ambiguous personifications save the Trinity were both morally unacceptable and categorically harmful... For Christians, an all-knowing god cannot be moved by mimesis; transformation through visual perfor-

> mance and supernatural omniscience must remain antithetical. For the Middle Ages, the body itself became a persona—a mask that its wearer only escaped at death.

According to Bharat Gupt,[13] "While Christianity established the notion of mask as evil disguise, the philosophy of scientific materialism, which defined reality in objective terms and which geared the concept of mimesis towards verisimilitude, redefined mask as untruth." It is only in the last century, with the breakdown of materialism as the basis of physics, and the rediscovery of the inner world that modern man's sensibility has become receptive to ancient artistic expression, making ancient ritual more accessible.

If the ancient secular theatre used masks and other symbols, so did the sacred theatre. Hindu communities in India and Bali still use masks in religious performance.

Indian ritual also involves a specialized vocabulary with layers of meaning and a deliberate use of paradox. Here words serve as masks. We see the continuation of such usage in the poetry of the medieval saints of India, where this language was called sandhyā-bhāṣā.

Asuric and Proper Readings of Sacrifice

We must be cautious and not read the descriptions of ritual literally. The ritual books have enough warnings about the paradoxical aspects of the performance in their own description.

Sacrifice allows the participant to bridge the divide of the body and the spirit and be transformed. But to the outsider the performance can be viewed in asuric (āsuri) terms or correctly (daivika). The asuric reading is literal; the correct one transcends simple dichotomies.

This is stressed most clearly in Īśa Upaniṣad. One is enjoined not to consider either the material or the abstract spiritual reading the correct reading. Ritual requires performance and that is the material or the avidyā part of it, but that, in turn, becomes the ground for the transcendent meaning:

> He who knows at the same time both the spirit (saṃbhūti) and the destruction (vināśa), overcomes death by destruction and obtains immortality through the spirit. (IU 14)

Unfortunately, to a beginner trying to understand the Vedic system, the asuric position appears most natural. This is responsible for much misunderstanding of Vedic rites and their meaning.

Let me add that the Chāndogya warns us about those who do not understand that the rite is about paradox and regeneration, and not the actual mechanics of the theatre. It compares the ritual of such people, who look only at the outer performance, to the udgītha of the dogs. This is what Vaka Dālbhya (also called Glāva Maitreya) saw of the dog-udgītha (CU 1.12):

> A white (dog) appeared, and other dogs gathering around him, asked, "Sir, sing and get us food, we are hungry."
>
> The white dog said to them, "Come to me tomorrow morning."
>
> The dogs came on, holding together, each dog keeping the tail of the preceding dog in his mouth, as the priests do when they are going to sing praises with the Vahiṣpavamāna hymn. After they had settled down, they began to say Hiṅ.
>
> "Om, let us eat! Om, let us drink!"

The dangers of misreading a highly symbolic language were recognized. The Purāṇas warn that the asuras copy whatever the devas do, and do it to a grander scale.

3

Animal Sacrifice

Was the original sacrifice real, and the symbolic enactment came later? Historians of religion have assumed that this is the order in which ritual evolved. But if one looks at non-Indic religions, we don't see that such a transition has always taken place. The Śatapatha Brāhmaṇa says that prior to King Śyāparṇa Sāyakāyana sacrifice of several animals actually took place (SB 6.2.1.39), but now it is limited only to the goat (aja). SB 3.2.2.9 also says that Agni is sacrifice personified and "only vegetation is proper for sacrifice; men could not have performed sacrifice without vegetation, thus only vegetation is appropriate for a sacrifice." In SB 6.2.1.29, it is stated that the *aja* sacrifice includes all the animals.

How about the symbolic sacrifice in the West? The symbolic sacrifice of Christ in the Catholic service is not mystical in the same sense as the Vedic sacrifice. But there is some commonality which many scholars believe is a result of the borrowing by the Church from Indic and Mithraic sources.

Given that the Ṛgveda already has a fully-developed system of symbolic sacrifice, we cannot say that an evolution from real slaughter of animals to an abstract system took place. Two possibilities could be proposed to understand the history of ritual in India: (i) there were groups, outside of the Ṛgvedic people, who slaughtered animals during sacrifice, so that history of Indian ritual should be seen as an interaction between these two groups; (ii) an embellishment of the symbolic sacrifice in terms of the real killing emerged later. In time of the Brāhmaṇas, we see a tension between these two points of view in the narrative. The sacrifice of the horse in the Ṛgveda appears to have been symbolic, because there is no evidence in the text of other such slaughter.

Both the views that Vedic rites slaughtered animals, and that the sacrifice was entirely symbolic, were current in medieval India. Those who believed in the reality of the killing of animals argued that violence is a fact of nature and a ritual enactment of violence is clear in a literal reading of the texts. In further support they quoted passages such as the Mahābhārata 12.5, where it is stated:

> I see no being which lives in the world without violence. Creatures exist at the mercy of one another; the strong consume the weak. The mongoose eats mice, just as the cat eats the mongoose. The dog kills the cat, and wild beasts eat the dog. Man eats them all. Everything that moves and is still is food for someone.

The opponents of this view did not contest the reality of violence, but they argued that the ritual is not about reality but rather an enactment of death and regeneration. In such a performance an actual death would weaken the force of the ritual. Furthermore, they argued, the texts, if read carefully, show that substitutes for animals were used.

They pointed out that the texts are to be read with care. The texts tell us *parokṣa iva priyā hi devāḥ, pratyakṣa dviṣaḥ*, the gods love what is paradoxical and detest what is obvious. The literal reading is for the asuras, whereas the devas are supposed to consider the deeper meaning. The Nirukta says *bahubhaktivādīni hī brāhmaṇāni*, words in the Brāhmaṇas have several meanings.

A performance of ritual, like any powerful narrative, must have a crisis. Since ritual deals with regeneration, it must involve transformation. This may be done by an actual offering of the life of an animal by an asura, but the more powerful enactment of this offering can only be symbolic. Fire is repeatedly called an animal in Vedic ritual, which is why it is used ubiquitously.

The ritualists believe that the whole world is connected. SB 6.2.1 describes how Agni saw the five forms—the man (puruṣa), the horse, the bull, the ram, and the he-goat. And since he saw (*paś*) them, they are called *paśu*. Man inheres in him all other animals. The ultimate sacrifice is of man himself for his ritual rebirth, but this can be substituted by the sacrifice of horse, bull, ram, and he-goat (SB 6.2.1.15).

The evidence from Śatapatha Br. 6.2.1.36-39 indicates that in sacrifice some people substituted a clay or gold image of the victim, although the author of the Brāhmaṇa disapproves of this substitution. Other authorities, such as Baudhāyana (BShS 22.1) and Aupamanyava (AShS 16.6.2) in the Śrauta Sūtras, consider it proper to use artificial or golden iconic heads in place of the real animals.

The Atharvaveda (7.5.4-5) says that the inner yajña is superior to the outer one:

> *yatpuruṣeṇa haviṣā yajñam devā atanvat*
> *asti nu tasmādojīyo yad vihavyenejire*
>
> Sages (deva, men) do sacrifice with puruṣa for oblation; more glorious than that is the sacrifice without oblation (i.e. inner sacrifice).
>
> *mugdhā devā uta śunāyajantota goraṅgaiḥ purudhāyajanta*
> *ya imam yajñam manasā ciketa pra ṅo vocastamiheha bravaḥ*
>
> Bewildered sages (men) sacrifice variously with dog, limbs of knowledge (or cow); he who knows with the mind this sacrifice–him we proclaim here, may you speak.

According to the Aitareya Brāhmaṇa 2.19:

> *sa vā eṣa paśurevaālabhyate yatpuroḍāśaḥ. tasya yāni kiṃśārūṇi tāni romāṇ, ye tuṣāḥ sā tvak, ye*

> *phalīkaraṇāstadsṛk, yat piṣṭam kiknasāḥ tanmāṃsam, yat kim citkam sāram tadasthi. sarveṣām vā eṣa paśūnām medhena yajate yaḥ puroḍāśena yajate. tasmādāhuḥ puroḍāśasatram lokyamiti*

> The cake (which is offered) is the victim that is killed; the chaff of it is the hairs, the husks the skin, the polishings the blood, the pounded grains and fragments the flesh, whatever substantial the bone. With the sap of all animals he sacrifices who sacrifices with the cake. Therefore they say, "The cake offering is the people's sacrificial session."

The Mahābhārata mentions the sacrifice of the horse in 14.89, but it is followed in 14.90 by an account of how a sacrifice of powdered barley is superior to this sacrifice. Sections 14.91 and 14.92 say it is best to do sacrifice with grain that have been saved for three years. It is also enjoined that sacrifice should not cause any injury.[14]These descriptions that alternate between one of apparent sacrifice and where the animal is described as a cake or grain heightens the mystery and power of the rite.

Animals are renewed with the year. Birds get new feathers, the Sun becomes strong again. We expect the "animal sacrifices' to mark the year. This is corroborated by the Mahābhārata's reference to the holding of the rite on the full Moon of Caitra.[15]We have other evidence that this time marked the beginning of the new year.

Song Animals

The word Sāman connotes equality and balance. It is normally a song, with its various movements, sung out of the Sāmaveda. But the Sāman is more than just a vocal sequence; it is the harmony in change. The Chāndogya speaks of the

Sāmans of the Sun, the seasons, the worlds, the breathings, and so on.

The upward and downward movements of the Sāman may be seen as having five or seven parts, both of which are described in the Chāndogya Upaniṣad. Considering just the five-fold Sāman, the movements are hiṅkāra, prastāva, udgītha, pratihāra, and nidhana. The birth is represented by hiṅkāra, the first ascent by prastāva, udgītha is the zenith, pratihāra is the descent, and nidhana is the closure. "Rising, the Sun is the hiṅkāra; risen, he is the prastāva; at noon he is the udgītha; in the afternoon he is the pratihāra; setting, he is the nidhana" (CU 2.14.1).

But these five movements are also the five animals of sacrifice (CU 2.6.1; 2.18.1):

> The hiṅkāra is goats, the prastāva sheep, the udgītha cows, the pratihāra horses, and the nidhana puruṣa.

The five sacrificial animals are the five movements of a sacred song! The specific identification may owe to etymological considerations and also to animal traits. Aja, goat, means the unborn; sheep climb up mountain sides; cow represents prosperity; horse is speed, appropriate for fast movement; and puruṣa is the objective of the song.

Seizing of animals is then no more than holding of specific movements of a Sāman.

Animals in the Sky

The sky was viewed in the ancient world as being populated by animals, which is why we speak of the Zodiac. The celestial Zoo has horses, sheep, goats, cows, and men – the five "animals" of sacrifice, together with a host of other animals. Mythology sums up astronomical knowledge in terms of stories of gods, kings, and heroes.[16] Such mythical knowledge is "rehearsed by symbolic experiences in the form of musical rites and performances involving the people... It is easier to respect than comprehend, but it leads to an idea of the overall texture of the cosmos."[17]

The Śatapatha 6.1 speaks of the creation of the universe by Prajāpati (star or abstract time), and in this creation Aśva, Rāsabha, Aja, and Kūrma come before the creation of the Earth. Clearly, these refer to stars or constellations. Their identification with the Sun (Aśva), Gemini (Rāsabha), Aja (Capricorn) and Kūrma (Cassiopeia) has been suggested.

This identification is supported by etymological considerations. RV 1.164.2 and Nirukta 4.4.27 define Aśva as the Sun. Rāsabha which literally means the twin asses are defined in Nighaṇṭu 1.15 as Aśvinau which later usage suggests are Castor and Pollux in Gemini. In Western astronomy the twin asses are to be found in the next constellation of Cancer as Asellus Borealis and Asellus Australis. Aja (goat) is defined by Nighaṇṭu 1.15 as a Sun and owing to the continuity that we see in the Vedic and later European names for constellations (as in the case of the Great Bear) it is reasonable to identify it as the constellation Capricorn (*caper* goat + *cornu* horn). Kūrma is a synonym of Kaśyapa (tortoise) which is linguistically close to Cassiopeia (from Greek Kassiopeia). Etymologically Kāśyapīya, slow like a tortoise, seems appropriate for Cassiopeia (from Greek Kassiopeia) since it is near the pole. This last name may point to an epoch when this constellation was even closer to the north pole.

Of the other sacrificial animals, cow is Vṛṣabha (Taurus), sheep is Meṣa (Aries), and man is Prajāpati (Orion). Through cosmic bandhu, the precessional motion of the stars finds voice in the Vedic chants and the drama of the "sacrifice."

4

Altars and Astronomy

Vedic ritual was performed at an altar, although it could be performed silently in the mind as well. The altar design was based on astronomical numbers related to the reconciliation of the lunar and solar years. Vedic rites mark the passage of time. The fire altars symbolize the universe and there are three types of altars representing the earth, the space and the sky (Figure 1). The altar for the earth is drawn as circular whereas the sky (or heaven) altar is drawn as square. The geometric problems of circulature of a square and that of squaring a circle are a result of equating the earth and the sky altars. We know these problems are among the earliest considered in ancient geometry.

The main sky altar was built in five layers in an expanded ritual ground (Figure 2), where the great Agnicayana rite was performed. The basic square shape was modified to several forms, such as falcon and turtle. The construction of these altars required the solution to several geometric and algebraic problems.

Agnicayana is one of the Soma sacrifices. The altar is generally made in the shape of the falcon, śyena or suparṇa. This construction is in five layers. Altars are made of bricks unless they are constructed symbolically of mantras. Bricks to be used in altar construction are classified into two types: ordinary, lokampṛṇā, and special, yajuṣmatī. Each yajuṣmatī brick is consecrated in a specific manner and each such brick is marked in a unique way. The very first brick to be consecrated is called aṣāḍhā; it is square, and it is marked with three lines (SB 6.5.3.2, TS 5.2.8.3). The square shape, we have noted before, represents heaven, while the three marks

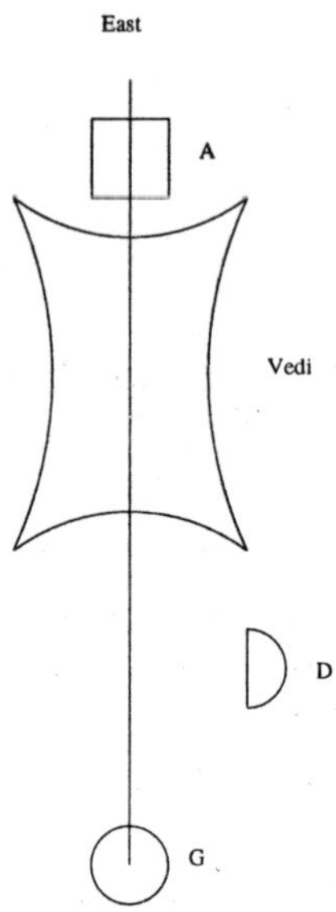

Figure 1: The ritual ground

represent the tripartite bandhu, or the triple nature of the universe. Bricks are built in different shapes to different measurements.

ŚB 10.4.3.14-20 describes the total number of yajuṣmatī bricks to be 396. This was to be taken as 360 days of the year and 36 additional (including one being the fillings between the bricks) as the days of the intercalary month. By layers, the first has 98, the second has 41, the third has 71, the fourth has 47, and the fifth has 138 (ŚB 10.4.3.14-18). The sum of the bricks in the fourth and the fifth layers refer to the 186 (together with the one space filling) tithis in the half-year. The number of bricks in the third and the fourth layers equals the integer nearest to one third the number of days in the lunar year. The number of bricks in the third layer equals the integer nearest to one fifth of the number of days in the lunar year. The number of bricks in the second and the third layers equals one third the number of days in a nakṣatra year of $28 \times 12 = 336$ days. Once the basic number of 21 is

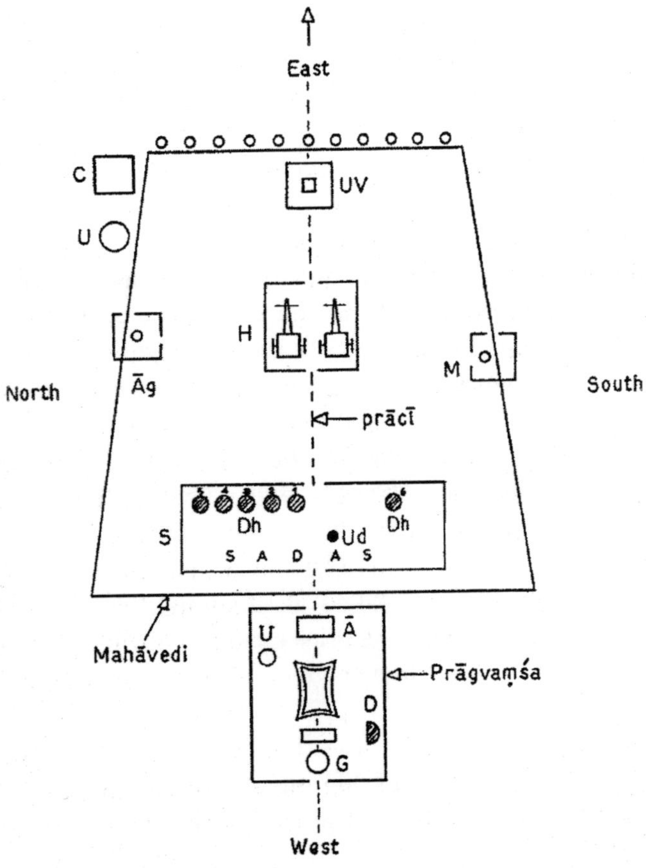

Figure 2: The expanded ritual ground. Ā: Āhavanīya; G: Gārhapatya ; D: Dakṣiṇāgni; UV: Uttaravedi; Dh: Dhiṣṇya hearths which inclu de Āg: Āgnīdhra and M: Mārjālīya; H: Havirdhāna shed

subtracted from the number of bricks in the first layer, the sum of the remainder together with the bricks in the second layer are once again the integer nearest one third the number of days in the lunar year.

The total lumber of lokampṛṇā bricks is 10,800 which equals the number of muhūrtas in a year (1 day = 30 muhūrtas), or equivalently the number of days in 30 years. Of these 21 go into the gārhapatya, 78 into the eight dhiṣṇya hearths, and the rest go into the āhavanīya altar.

The fire altars are surrounded by 360 enclosing stones (pariśrita), of these 21 are around the gārhapatya, 78 around the dhiṣṇya, and 261 around the āhavanīya (ŚB 10.4.3.13). The āhavanīya includes the dhiṣṇya, therefore the number of days assigned exclusively to the āhavanīya is 261-78= 183 days, which is equal to the days in the uttarāyaṇa of a 366 day year. The choice of the 21 days for the gārhapatya is from the unique symbolism of this number. It is also the sum of the first six integers. Once the numbers 21 and 183 are chosen the number 78 becomes the only choice for the dhiṣṇya. This number 78 is the sum of the first twelve integers.

The dhiṣṇya hearths are in one layer in a size of 18 aṅgulas in either a square or circular form. The number of enclosing stones equals the number of bricks used in a dhiṣṇya hearth, and these are 8 each for five of them with the remaining three using 6, 11, and 21.

The main altar was an area that was taken to be equivalent to the nominal year of 360 days. Now, each subsequent year, the shape was to be reproduced with the area increased by one unit.

Several kinds of year are mentioned: (i) nākṣatra of 324 days, which is 12 times 27 nakṣatras; (ii) nākṣatra of 336 days, which is 12 times 28 nakṣatras; (iii) lunar, which is a fraction more than 354 days (360 tithis); and (iv) solar, which is in excess of 365 days (between 371 and 372 tithis).

The Ṛgveda itself was taken to symbolize the universe, so the altar numbers show up in its organization. The verse count of the Ṛgveda is the number of *sky* days in forty years

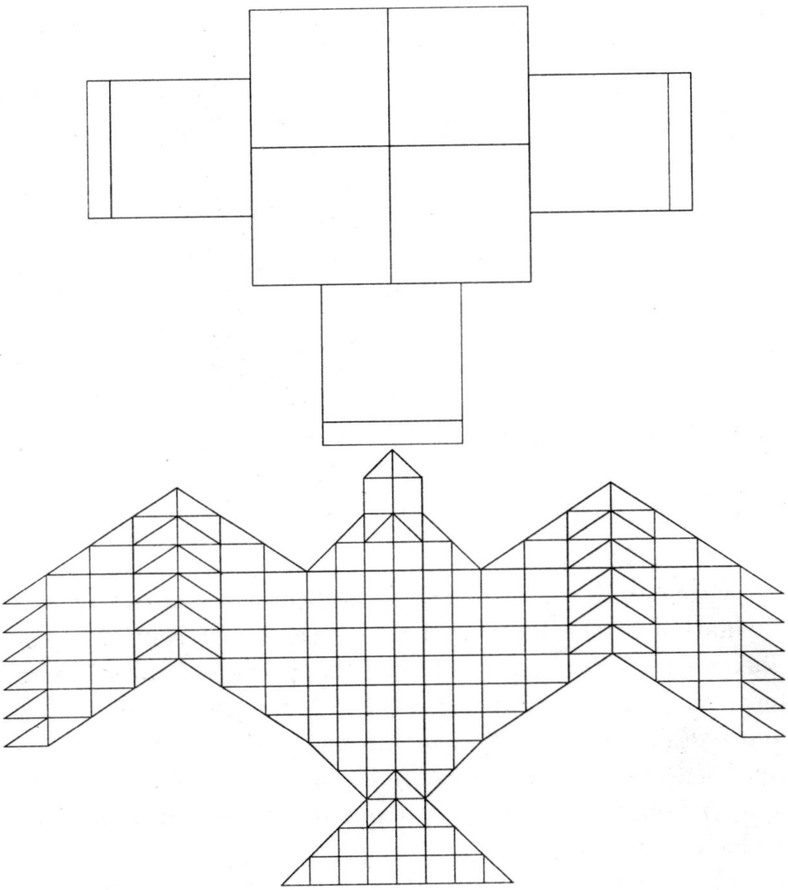

Figure 3: The basic bird altar (top); the bird altar in the shape of an eagle (śyenacit)

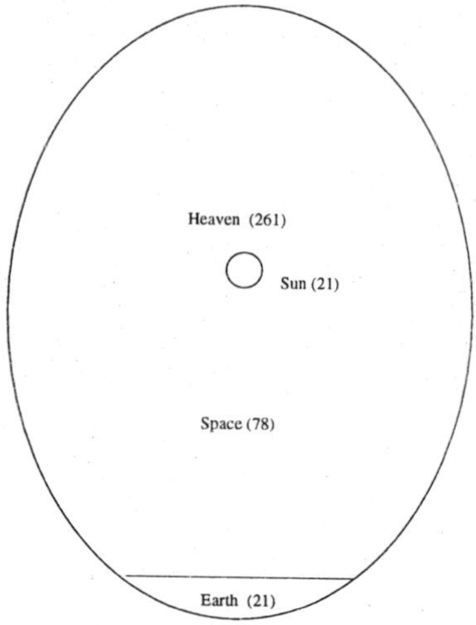

Figure 4: The subjective cosmos with its three divisions of earth (body), atmosphere (prāṇa), and sky (consciousness).

or $261 \times 40 = 10,440$, and the verse count of all the Vedas is $261 \times 78 = 20,358$.

Although in Agnicayana, the altar design relates to a reconciliation of the lunar and solar years, representing outer phenomena, The lunar and the solar processes are taken to have analogs within the individual. Therefore, Vedic rites mark the passage of time within and without. The subjective cosmos may be shown as in Figure 3. The connections of it to the outer cosmos make it possible to obtain knowledge by looking within.

The layers of the altar have the following significance: The first layer represents the earth, the third the space, and the fifth the sky. The second layer represents the joining of the earth and space, whereas the fourth layer represents the joining of space and sky. This altar was symbolically represented as a falcon (Figure 4) or a tortoise as well as other shapes.

The identification of the year and man was carried on beyond the identity of 360 days and 360 bones. The Śatapatha

Br. (12.3.2.5) speaks of the year having 10,800 muhūrtas (1 muhūrta = 48 minutes), and the basic Agnicayana altar was to have an area of 108,000 square aṅgulas.

5

The Aśvamedha Rite

To see this rite in perspective, note that five great sacrifices (pañca-mahāyajña), also to be viewed as remembrance and worship, are prescribed for all people. These are to be done daily and consist of:

1. *Brahmayajña,* the remembrance of Brahman, the Spirit, by reciting the Vedas.

2. *Pitṛyajña,* the remembrance of the ancestors.

3. *Devayajña,* remembering gods by pouring ghee on the sacred fire.

4. *Bhūtayajña,* remembering to scatter grain and other food on the threshold for animals and birds.

5. *Puruṣayajña,* worship of men, by showing them hospitality.

Each sacrifice belongs to a larger matrix of ceremonies. How this system of sacrifices expanded to include the royal sacrifices is explained in the Aitareya Brāhmaṇa. AB 1.14 speaks of how the devas thought of kingship in order to defeat the asuras, with whom their conflict was not going well. The consecration of the king was done by Rājasūya, and its further rejuvenation by the Vājapeya and the Aśvamedha sacrifices.

The Aśvamedha is performed by a consecrated king, who is assisted by his four wives, the Mahiṣī (the senior queen), the Vāvātā (the favorite), the Parivṛktā, and the Pālāgalī. The Mahiṣī is addressed by the Brahmin, the Vāvātā by the Udgātṛ, the Parivṛktā by the Hotṛ, and the Pālāgalī by the kṣattṛ. These four queens are served by hundred daughters

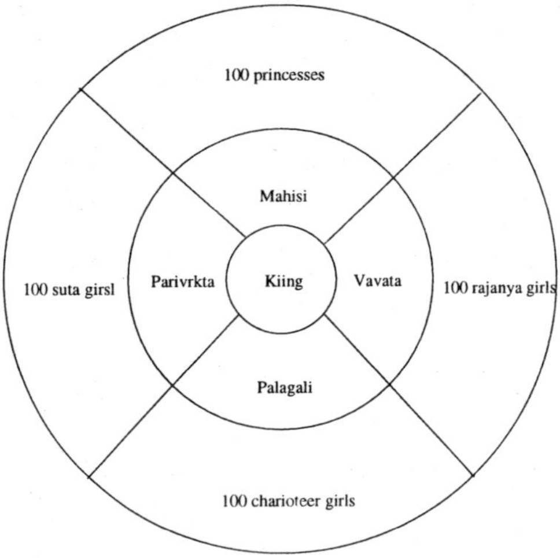

Figure 5: The king, the queens, and their attendants

each of the rājās, the rājanyas, the sūtas and the grāmaṇīs, and the kṣattṛs and the saṃgrahītṛs, respectively (Figure 5).

Since one would not expect every king, desirous of performing this rite, to have four wives, this number is merely emphasizes the four-fold classification of the world that forms the basis of this rite. This classification indicates that all the classes of subjects are equal participants in it. The description is normative and it is clear that modifications to it could be made.

The description of the sacrifice starts thus:

> The Aśvamedha is a three-day Soma sacrifice. It is done in spring. Six or seven days before the full Moon of Phālguna, the four priests, the Adhvaryu, the Hotṛ, the Brahmin, and the Udgātṛ meet. The Adhvaryu cooks a rice meal for the four. The Sacrificer (King) presents the rice meal and gold plates to the priests. The four queens are in attendance. The horse is "purified" for the rite using darbha stalks. (SB 13.4.1-8, 13.1.1.1-2)

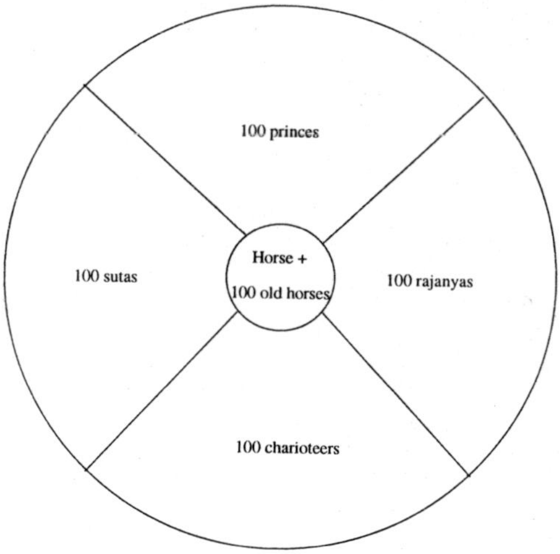

Figure 6: The horse and its attendants

The symbolism of rice is that it represents the seed (by extension that of Time or Sun, Horse), as does gold.

The horse, who is black in the forepart, white in the backpart, and which has a mark on its forehead, is set free to roam anywhere for a year. The horse is protected by 400 soldiers, and the regions where it goes are claimed by the monarch. The 400 soldiers include: 100 royal princes clad in armour; 100 warriors armed with swords; 100 sons of heralds and headsmen, bearing quivers filled with arrows; 100 sons of attendants and charioteers, bearing staves; and 100 exhausted, worn-out horses which act as companions to the sacrificial horse and guard it (Figure 6). It is noteworthy that none of the soldiers is mounted. The addition of 100 horses to the already enumerated four categories of soldiers indicates that the animals also have a share in the rite.

The parallels between Figures 5 and 6 are striking. The horse is surrounded by 100 old horses; the king is likewise surrounded by a multitude of councillors. According to the Pañcaviṃśa Brāhmaṇa, eight of these councillors are particularly close to him:

> Eight important persons sustain together the kingship: the king's brother, the king's son, the purohita, the queen, the sūta, the grāmaṇī, the kṣattṛ, and the charioteer. (PB 19.1.4)

These eight can be put into four classes of two each.

This four-fold classification is related to the creation of the universe by the Puruṣa by his primal sacrifice. That sacrifice created four classes of social order; it also created three kinds of beasts: those who live in the air, in the forests, and in villages. Horse, has a unique position: it is the sky-bird; it lives in the forest, and in the village. According to RV 10.90:

> Horses were born from [the Puruṣa], and those other animals that have two rows of teeth; cows were born from him, and from him were born goats and sheep.
>
> When they divided the Puruṣa, into how many parts did they apportion him? What do they call his mouth, his two arms and thighs and feet?
>
> His mouth became the brahmin; his arms were made into the rājanya; his thighs the vaiśya, and from his feet the śudra was born.
>
> The Moon was born from his mind; from his eye the Sun was born. Indra and Agni came from his mouth, and from his vital breath the Wind was born.
>
> From his navel the middle region of space arose; from his head the sky emerged. From his two feet came the earth, and the quarters of the sky from his ear. Thus they set the world in order.

As a representation of the cosmos, the classes of people are to be viewed as being integrated, all part of the web of creation. Each person is in the image of the Puruṣa, so he has elements of the brahmin, the rājanya, the vaiśya, and the śudra in him. Likewise, the king inheres in himself all the classes, so to rejuvenate the kingdom all four classes should participate in the ritual.

Twenty-one stakes are fixed on the ground. The horse is tied to the central stake. A detailed description of the stakes is in SB 13.4.4. The central stake is of rajjudāla wood. Flanking it are two pitudāru stakes, one on each side. These in turn are flanked by 6 bilva-wood stakes, three on each side. Outside of these are 6 khadira-wood stakes, three on each side; and outermost of all, are 6 palāśa stakes.

These 21 stakes are thus in the image of the universe: the central stake is the nose, the pitudāru stakes are the eyes, the bilva stakes are the marrow, the khadira stakes are the bones, and the palāśa stakes are the flesh of this Prajāpati.

Twelve other animals (paryaṅgas) are tied to the body of the horse. These apart, the central stake has 17 animals, and the other 20 stakes have 16 animals tied to each. These are all domestic (grāmya) animals. In the 20 spaces between the 21 stakes are tied wild animals, 13 to each location. Thus a total of 337 domestic animals and 260 wild animals are tied to the stakes and the gaps. The stakes are eight-cornered. The whole arrangement is as shown in Figure 7.

Now occurs the sacrifice of the horse. Likewise, the other domestic animals are sacrificed. The wild animals are set free at the end of the ceremony.

If one looks at the evidence from RV 1.162.2-4 and 1.163.12, it appears that only two victims, a he-goat and the horse are sacrificed, so the accounts of the Ṛgveda and the Śatapatha are not identical.

The horse represents prāṇa, the Sun, time, and the universe. The fact that the horse has 34 ribs (RV 1.162.18), equaling the count of 27 nakṣatras, along with five planets, and the Sun and the Moon, makes it an appropriate symbol

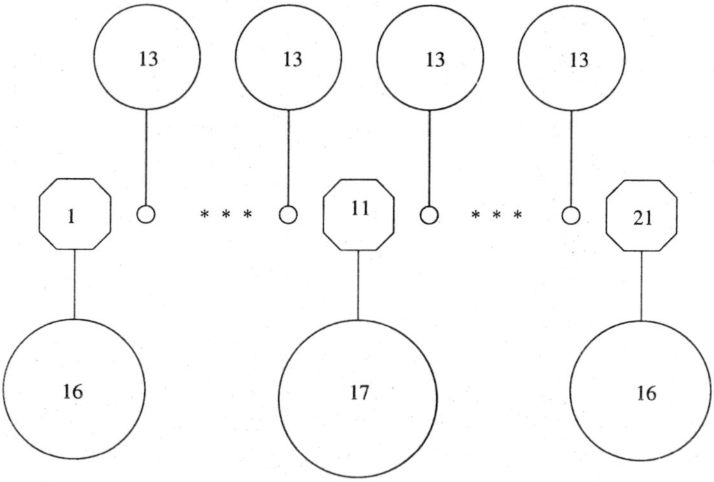

Figure 7: The stakes to which the animals are tied; the circles below represent the domestic animals, the circles above represent the wild animals; the sacrificial horse is tied to the central stake, number *11*

for the universe. The Aśvamedha rite is to transcend Time.

It is useful to compare this rite to the Rājasūya rite, which is to celebrate the regeneration of the royal power, to reconsecrate him. In the words of J.C. Heesterman:[18]

> Ascension and descent, disintegration and reintegration, chaotic dispersion and re-articulated structure, such are the terms of the cosmic rhythm as represented in the different phases of the rājasūya... [T]he unction exemplifies the cosmic role of the king; on the joint between two time cycles, having encompassed and articulated the universe during the course of the preceding time cycle, he emerges from his dīkṣā, that is his embryonic state, to be born; but at the same time he dies and disintegrates, to ripen during another year-long dīkṣā (or to be recomposed by a course through the universe) towards a new birth at the

> end of the next time cycle when the same process starts all over again. In other words, the king, as represented in the rājasūya, is the incorporation of the universe's moving forces: "boom to bust, and boom again."

In exactly the same spirit, the Aśvamedha is to regenerate time itself for the sake of royal regeneration.

Initiation

In the beginning, a "four-eyed dog" (a dog with markings above its eyes) is made to float under the sacrificial horse (SB 13.1.2.9), who is worth a thousand cows (SB 13.4.2.1). The four eyes here indicate markings on top of the eyes. The "four-eyed dog" is Sirius, the Dog star, the brightest light of Canis Major, whose orbit is below (to the south) that of the Sun.[19]The four eyes are the Mirzam, Furud, γ, and η.

The ascent of the Sun puts an end to the light of Sirius, the brightest star in the sky. The reference to the thousand cows is about the Sun's splendour being a thousand times that of the Earth, since gauḥ also means the planet. The first step of the initiation mirrors sunrise.

Twenty-one stakes are fixed to the ground. On the second Soma-day, there is mention of binding of the horse, a hornless he-goat, and a gomṛga to the central stake. Fifteen more animals (paryaṅgas) are tied to the horse, so that the total number of animals tied to the central stake is 17. Each of the remaining 20 stakes has 16 animals tied to it. A total of 337 animals are bound to the stakes.

Now is a mention of three kinds of "slaughtering knives." The knife for the horse is made of gold, that for the paryaṅga animals is made of copper, and that for the remaining ones is made of iron. This represents a three-fold division of the universe. The horse is the Sun, the paryaṅga animals are the space, and the remaining animals are the earth.

The significance of the count of 21 for the stakes is that

this number also represents the Sun (SB 13.3.3.3; 13.5.1.5); in fact, the Sun is called ekaviṃśa.

The Adhvaryu sprinkles some water on the horse (SB 13.2.7.1). There is mention of "killing" of the horse (SB 13.2.8.2), and the leading of the queens to the horse with the formula, "Ambā, Ambikā, Ambālikā." The queens circle the horse six times (SB 13.2.8.4).

Three kinds of needles are now used on the sacrificed horse: gold, copper, and iron, to soften the different regions of the horse, upper, intermediate, and general.

Now, the horse, after being cleansed is led up. *Later he is set free.* Two lute-players sing in praise of the king and the sacrificial ritual (SB 13.4.3.3-5). One of these is a brahmin and the other is a rājanya; this is a play on the theme of opposition and balance. The players provide music on several occasions.

The priests invoke and praise the householders, the Fathers, the atharvans, the apsarases, the snake charmers, the rākṣases, the asurās, fish and fishermen, birds and birdcatchers, and the śrotriyas. During the period of the ceremonies, an Agnicayana altar is also constructed (Figure 3). For the construction of this altar very many bricks of different designs are used.

But how long is the horse supposed to be free? In later enactment of the ritual, the horse roamed for one year (varṣa). But the Ṛgvedic and the Śatapatha accounts suggest that the rite took place just over a few days. It appears, therefore, that the original meaning was to consider the day of the Sun as symbolic of its annual circuit. Such usage across levels is very commonly employed in the Indian texts.

The time spent by the queen with the "dead horse" (aśvaka) was the time spent with a fire called aśvaka,[20] which represented the Sun dead in the sky during the night, preserved in a small sized fire on the earth.

The prototype of this sacrifice must have been for everyone, but as the pageantry associated with it expanded, it could be afforded only by a king.

Forms and Names

To consider the significance of ritual formulae, consider SB 11.2.3, where it is argued that the universe is completely described only when we realize its transcendental aspect. Furthermore, the element of naming is fundamental to mastery. The sacrifice, by confronting the question of of the nature of time, as symbolized in the image of the horse, provides a path to the glory of the king and his subjects:

> In the beginning, this universe was the Brahman. It created the gods; and having created the gods, it made them ascend these worlds: Agni this earth, Vāyu the air, and Sūrya the sky.
>
> And the deities who are above these he made ascend the worlds which are above these; and, indeed, just as these (three) worlds and these (three) deities are manifest, so are those (higher) worlds and those (higher) deities manifest—(the worlds) which he made those deities ascend.
>
> Then the Brahman itself went up to the sphere beyond. Having gone up to the sphere beyond, it considered, "How can I descend again into those worlds?" It then descended again by means of these two—Form and Name. Whatever has a name, that is name; and that again which has no name, and which one knows by its form, "This is (of a certain) form," that is form: as far as there are Form and Name so far, indeed, extends this (universe).
>
> These, indeed, are the two great forces of the Brahman; and, verily, he who knows these two great forces of the Brahman becomes himself a

> great force. (SB 11.2.3)

It is this transcendence that leads to the paradoxical aspects of the sacrifice. Since the transcendence aspect penetrates all forms, it becomes possible to represent one form by another.

Quieting the Horse

As the finale of the sacrifice approaches, the animals are recounted. In addition, there is mention of the seizing of three kapiñjalas for spring, three sparrows for summer, and three partridges for the rainy season.

Now a cloth, upper cloth is spread and some gold placed on it. The horse is "quieted" (SB 13.5.2), after being made to lay down on the cloth. The four queens, a young maiden, and four hundred attendants arrive to wash the feet.

The first queen (*mahiṣī*) now lays down near the horse, and she is covered up with the upper cloth. There is a scripted dialogue between the priests, the maiden, and the queens. At the end of the dialogue they walk back, and the others sing from RV 4.39.6:

> Dadhikrāvan walks in the front with the ranks of the leading chariots of the asuras. He is bedecked like a horse, raising dust behind him, chewing on the reins.

Dadhikrāvan is just another name of the Sun. RV 4.39.8 says that the asuras are as afraid of Dadhikrāvan as are fighters of the thunderbolt (vajra). Brahmāṇḍa Purāṇa 4.1.58 describes Dadhikrāvan as a Marīci deva in the Rohita Manavantara. This indicates a reference to the Inner Sun.

Although the subsequent description of the sacrifice speaks of the omenta (vapā), it is not clear that the horse has actually been killed. The word vapā is defined in SB 6.3.3.5 by *valmīkavapā*, or vapā is a termite hill. This identity of the omenta with the vapā has an interesting basis in the symbolism described in the Chāndogya Upaniṣad. In the five-fold

Sāman, pratihāra is horse; in the seven-fold Sāman, pratihāra is germs (and termite) (CU 2.6.1 and 2.9.1). Further, note that after an earlier similar description of the initiatory rites, we found the horse set free to roam for a year.

Brahmodaya

There are two brahmodayas — philosophical exchanges — in the course of the rite. In the first one, between the Brahmin and the Hotṛ, the mantras of VS 23.9-12, which are in a question-answer form, are repeated in a consolidated order (SB 13.2.6.10-16):

> Who is it that walks alone? It is the Sun that walks alone; and he is spiritual lustre. Spiritual lustre the two (priests) bestow on him (the sacrificer).
>
> Who is born again? It is the Moon that is born again and again. (Moon's) vitality they bestow on him.
>
> What counters the cold? Agni counters the cold; its fiery spirit they bestow on him.
>
> What is the great vessel? The Earth is doubtless the great vessel. (By knowing it the sacrificer) establishes himself (upon it).
>
> What was the first conception? The first conception was doubtless the sky, rain—these two he secures for himself.
>
> Who was the great bird? The great bird, doubtless, was the horse—its vital powers he secures for himself.

> Who was the smooth one? The smooth one, doubtless, was beauty—beauty he thus secures for himself.

The second brahmodaya occurs immediately after the sacrifice is complete and it involves all priests. It uses mantras from VS 23.45-62 onwards (SB 13.5.2.12-21). I present only the actual questions and their answers:

> Who is that walks alone?
> —The Sun walks alone.
>
> What lustre is equal to the Sun?
> —The Brahman is the light equal to the Sun.
>
> Has Viṣṇu entered the universe at those three places where he is worshiped?
> —I pervade those three steps in which resides the whole universe. With one limb, I go around the earth and the sky, and beyond the sky.
>
> Into what things has the Puruṣa entered, and what things are established in the Puruṣa?
> —Into five things has the Puruṣa entered, and they are established in the Puruṣa.
>
> Who was the first conception?
> —The sky was the first conception.
>
> Who is the tawny one? Who moves in leaps? Who is the kurupiśaṅgilā? Who creeps along the path?
> —The tawny one is the uncreated (night); the kurupiśaṅgilā is the porcupine; the hare move in leaps, and the snake creeps along the path.

> How many kinds are there of this sacrifice, how many syllables? How many oblations, how often is the fire enkindled? How many priests worship?
> —Six kinds there are of this sacrifice, a hundred syllables, eighty oblations and three kindling-sticks, seven priests officiate.

> Who knows the navel of this universe, and of heaven and earth and air? Who knows the birthplace of the great Sun? Who knows the Moon, and whence it was born? —I know the navel of this universe; I know heaven and earth and air; I know the birthplace of the great Sun; and I know the Moon, and whence it was born.

> I ask you about the farthest end of the earth. I ask where is the navel of the universe. I ask you about the seed of the vigorous Time (*Aśva*). I ask you about the highest seat of speech.
> —This altar-ground is the farthest end of the earth; this sacrifice is the navel of the universe; this Soma is the seed of the vigorous Time; this Brahman is the highest seat of speech.

Gifts

The gifts are given preserving the four-fold theme running through the rite. The four priests, Hotṛ, Brahmin, Adhvaryu, and Udgātṛ, who are classified according to the directions east, south, west, and north, respectively, claim gifts lying in their directions (SB 13.5.4.24).

At the closing offering four women, with a maiden as the fifth, and four hundred female attendants are given (SB 13.5.4.27). This narrative simply presents the equation with the king, the four queens, and the 400 attendants in mirror image (Figure 8).

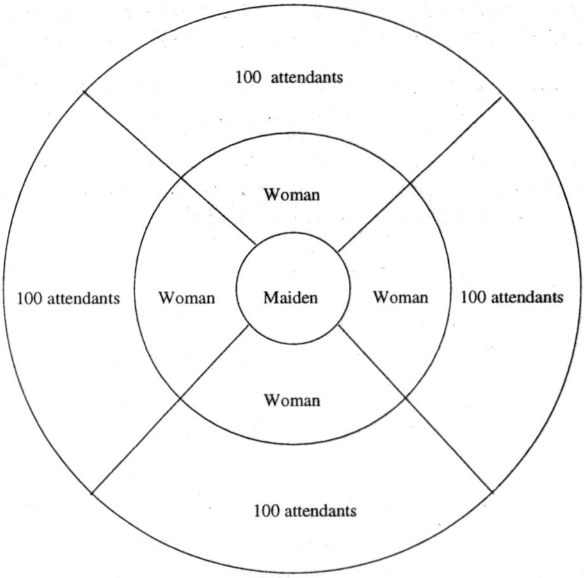

Figure 8: The "gifts" to the priests

Gifts bind the participants in a social embrace. The officiants of the sacred theatre gain materially in exchange for the magic that they have created that transforms the spirits of the others. This transformation is made complete by the invocation of all type of gods.

The relationship of the directions to the gods is described variously. Here, we follow the Chāndogya 3.6-10 according to which Vasu and Agni reside in the east, Rudra and Indra in the south, Āditya and Varuṇa in the west, and Maruta and Soma in the north. In the center is the Sādhya, the Sacrificer, with the Brahman in his head.

6

Domestic and Wild Beasts

What is the role of the dichotomy of the domestic and the wild beasts in the ritual? These two classes mirror the dichotomy of the king (who represents order) and the brahmin (who represents the limitless potential of the spiritual power). The paradox underlying the dichotomy is that if the king were to exercise absolute control the people will be unhappy, there will be no creativity, the gods will frown, and the kingdom will lose its prosperity. On the other hand, if the purohita were to become dominant, the ritual will lose its spiritual basis and the society will become āsuric. The resolution to this paradox was the sacrifice (abandonment) of material wealth by the purohita. We will discuss the king-purohita dichotomy further in the next session.

Regarding animals, the king may wish to have only domestic animals, but their health and well-being depends on the existence of the forest and its dwellers. This necessitates the need for balance between the wild and the tame. The wild beasts cannot be sacrificed, but we must acknowledge them. But this acknowledgement does not solve the conundrum underlying the division. According to SB 13.2.4:

> Prajāpati desired, "Would that I might gain both worlds, the world of the gods, and the world of men." He saw those beasts, the tame and the wild ones; he seized them, and by means of them took possession of these two worlds. By means of the tame beasts he took possession of this (terrestrial) world, and by means of the wild beasts of yonder (world); for this world is the world of men, and yonder world is the world of the gods...

> Would he to complete (the sacrifice) with tame ones, the roads would run together, the villages would be contiguous, and no ogres, man-tigers, thieves, murderers, and robbers would come to be in the forests. By (so doing) with wild (beasts), the roads would get disconnected, the villages would be too far apart, and there would come to be [too many] ogres, man-tigers, thieves, murderers, and robbers in the forests...
>
> He completes (the sacrifice) with tame (beasts),—father and son part company, the roads run together, the villages become contiguous, and no ogres, man-tigers, thieves, murderers, and robbers come to be in the forests.

SB 5.4.4.8-10 has an interesting account of the origin of the wild animals. The story is about Indra who, ordinarily, is our senses. Since these senses are generally scattered, Indra is shown to have a thousand orifices. When he drinks Soma, which is a statement of his dissociation from the normal state, he can lose control of his lower senses. From these lower ones, wild animals were born: "From the lower opening wild beasts sprang, with the tiger as their foremost."

Seven Song Animals

The Chāndogya speaks of a seven-fold Sāman where the animal identification is more elaborate than the one that was mentioned in the Introduction. Here the seven movements are called hiṅkāra, prastāva, saṅgava, udgītha, pratihāra, upadrava, and nidhana.

> Let a man meditate on the seven-fold Sāman as the Sun. The Sun is Sāman, because he is always the same (sama); he is Sāman because he is the same, everybody thinking, 'he looks towards me, he looks towards me.' (CU 2.9.1)

Hiṅkāra are the general animals (paśu), prastāva are men, saṅgava are the birds, udgiītha are the gods, pratihāra are the germs, upadrava are the wild animals, and nidhana are the ancestors. The domestic and the wild animals fall on opposite sides of udgītha here.

The domestic animals are the rising movements of the Sāman, and the wild animals are its descending movements.

Different Numbers

Several numbers are part of the rite. These are symbolic representations of different notions that are explained in the Śatapatha and other Brāhmaṇas. For example, 17 is assigned to Prajāpati; 16 and 13 represent domestic and wild animals, respectively. In BU 3.9, it is stated that there are 33 gods. Since Prajāpati transcends them, he is the 34th. Domestic animals, since they are not quite in the same league as the gods are symbolized by 32. From these two numbers emerge 17 and 16. SB 13.5.1.15 says about the number 13: "Thirteen wild beasts are seized for the year consists of thirteen months."

Another number of the sacrifice is 101. When the horse is being anointed, the queens weave 101 pearls into the mane on both sides and in the tail (SB 13.2.6.8), where the hair is likened to gold. It might be that this number mirrors the 101 nāḍīs of the heart (CU 8.6.6, KU 6.16-17) as the sacrificial horse represents the heart of the cosmos. The three places where the pearls are woven reflect the tripartite division of the universe and the sacrifice.

The three primary Aśvamedha numbers are 21, 260, and 337, the number of stakes, the number of wild animals, and the number of domestic animals (Figure 9). In addition, the 12 paryaṅga animals tied to the sacrificial horse represent the 12 months of the year, reinforcing the identity of the horse with the year, or more abstractly with time.

Out of these numbers, 21 represents the earth as well as the Sun. Perhaps, it represents the earthly rule of the king

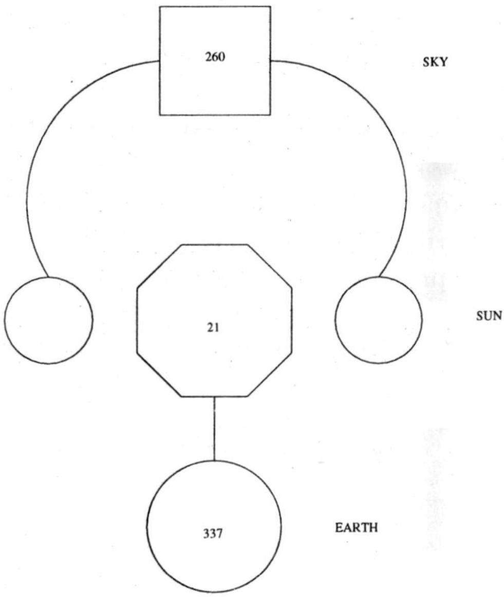

Figure 9: The domestic and the wild animals representing earth and the sky, whereas the stakes represent the Sun

who desires to mount the heaven in this life by acquiring the merit and fame of the sacrifice. The other two numbers are $260 = 261 - 1$ and $337 = 336 + 1$, which are one less than the sky number and one more than the nākṣatra year, respectively.

The horse represents an animal who straddles both the worlds of the heaven and earth. Quoting RV 10.1-2 and VS 21.43, SB 6.4.4.2 says this of the horse, " 'Thus born, you are the child of the two worlds,'—these two worlds, doubtless, are these two, heaven and earth." Agni is likewise the child of heaven and earth, and as the prototype paśu it is perfect to represent the horse.

The dual origin of the horse makes it perfect for mediation between the worlds of the forest and the village. So this excess of one amongst the domestic animals and one shortage amongst the wild ones might represent the loan from the wild (which represents the devas) to the domestic, to make the latter complete. Th equating of the sky and the earth represents also the lifting of the earth to the heaven. To put differently, it represents an ascension to the heaven, just as that idea forms part of the Rājasūya sacrifice also.[21]

7

The Authority of the King

Having examined the balance between the domestic and the wild animals, we come to the balance necessary between the king and his councillors. Indian kingship is not absolute and the king derives his power from the councillors, represented here by the brahmin. The king and the councillors mirror the dichotomy of the universe into the body and the spirit, or the earth and the sky. The two are fundamentally apart, but one cannot exist apart from the other.

One sees here several kinds of balance amongst the king and those who surround him. First, is the balance between the king's family and outsiders. There are the three king's relatives and his purohita on one side (if the purohita could be considered his ritual father), and the four charioteers, who represent the general populace. There is a balance between his wife (and son) and the brother, between the royalty and the commoners, and finally between the royal power and that of the power of the purohita. The king obtains his power from the araṇya where the āśramas of the gurus are located, and where also reside wild and dangerous animals and people. The araṇya is full of danger and opportunity. The king must build his strength in the araṇya to be able to rule the grāma. We see this pattern in the travails of Rāma and Yudhiśṭhira.

The basis of the balance is the four-fold division of function, which works at several levels, and also recursively. Since there are the four queens representing four directions, the guardians of these directions, Āpyas, Sādhyas, Anvādhyas, and Maruts, are invoked.

But these divisions cannot be static. There is the need for a tension that allows room for transcendence beyond the divisions. This tension is one of the undercurrents of the sacrifice.

In the tension between the domestic and the wild, only the domestic, by virtue of their symbolic sacrifice, are reborn. The purohita, who represents the brāhma power may be equated to the wild. The king does not hold absolute power; he must depend on the people (viś) and the authority of the purohita is a check on him. This creates a conundrum regarding the the king's authority. Heesterman describes it very eloquently in the following words:[22]

> [T]he achievement of transcendent authority, epochal as it was, was in a way a Pyrrhic victory, for in order to safeguard the transcendence of authority, the brahmin, though equally in need of the king's favors for his subsistence, was not allowed to serve the king and lend him his own authority, but had to keep himself from worldly entanglements and especially from being entangled in the king's affairs. Royal power and brahmanic authority were irredeemably divorced. This explains why ... there is no consistent theory of kingship: there cannot be one. The conflicting necessities of the cooperation between the king and the brahmin on the one hand and of their rigorous separation on the other demonstrate the irreducible character of the problem. Though this problem is not the sole property of India, it may be reckoned to be one of the achievements of Indian thought to have formulated in such exemplary fashion the ultimately insoluble conundrum of authority.

Although Heesterman considers this conundrum insoluble, the checks and balances working between the king, the purohita, the queen, and the other councillors creates the tension which is the solution to the problem.

The representation of the universe in the sacrifice required the ritualists to analyze clearly the social equations that form a society and the basis of the king's power. The ritual, for this reason, includes all classes of people; there is a representation of the animals also.

The question of the king's authority can also be seen through the dichotomy of asat and sat. Asat is the physical world, governed by the king, whereas sat is the transcendent world, the subject of the sacrifice. The sacrifice allows the king to renew his power by a momentary bridging of the two, but the two worlds remain apart.

This is seen most clearly in the announcement made at the consecratory soma feast for the king at the Rājasūya sacrifice (TS 1.8.10, VS 9.40): "This is your king, O Bhāratas," together with "but Soma is the king of us brahmins." There exist, after all, two powers: those of body and mind, and who commands the body can never be sure of the command of the mind.

The king is at the sacrifice a brahmin, subject to the authority of Soma. Nevertheless, he is being announced as the king of all people, which creates a situation filled with danger, paradox, and mystery. The king's power is renewed through the process of ritual death. In effect, the sacrifice delivers a new king.

8

Epilogue

The Aśvamedha rite is the ritual sacrifice of the Sun (time) to regenerate it. The narrative touches upon the inner and the outer Aśvas through the symbolism of the horse.

These ideas are described in SB 13.1.4 in the following manner: Prajāpati produced the Aśvamedha. It went straight away from him and spread itself over the regions. The gods went to search for it. By means of sacrifice they found it. Likewise the Sacrificer finds the horse with his rites. The horse disappears at night (the Sun has set), and that provides rest for the next day. The sacrifice seeks the horse the next day; it is lost again the next night. But the rite "brings about the security of possession" to the Sacrificer.

The enactment of this rite regenerates the powers and the fame of the king. When Indra's energies, or vital powers, departed from him, the gods restored them by means of sacrifice (SB 12.8.1.1). As a solar rite, one is enjoined to perform it year after year. Originally, it was done in Phālguna. The corresponding month for its enactment now will be the month of Pauṣa or perhaps Mārgaśīrṣa.

The number of animals used in this rite is related to the numerical symbolism associated with the earth, the atmosphere, and the heaven. These numbers also occur in the great Agnicayana rite, which is performed along with it. These numbers map the symbolic passage of the Sacrificer to the heaven, together with the similar passage of the "horse".

The rite can be performed at many different levels. The Śatapatha tells us that icons were used by some in place of the animals. According to the Chāndogya, the animals are the parts of a Sāman.

This rite is a variation on the basic solar theme that we find in other rites. For example, the Jyotiṣṭoma rite has been seen as the "appearance of the Sun out of darkness and the spread of cosmic light. The Sun's reaching heaven and the ascent to heaven of the sacrificer run parallel."[23]Sometimes this theme was transferred to the Moon, as in the Śatapatha 11.2.5.1 statement that the Aśvamedha is the Moon.

Chronological questions

The Śatapatha says that the year begins with the full Moon of Phālguna (SB 6.2.2.18), which is when the Aśvamedha was performed. On the other hand, in the Mahābhārata, the performance culminates on the full Moon of Caitra (Mb 14.76). The beginning of the year used in the Mahābhārata is different from the one in the Śatapatha. The seasons have shifted by a month, assuming the same reckoning of the year was employed during the Mahābhārata as in the earlier Brāhmaṇas.

The precession of the earth causes the months to shift with respect to seasons at a rate of about 2000 years per month, therefore a time-gap of about 2000 years exists between its descriptions in the Śatapatha and in the Mahābhārata. The word "precession" is from the fact that this circuit runs opposite to that of the normal sequence of months, so in the precessional shift, Caitra precedes Phālguna. The sequence of months is Vaiśākha, Jyaiṣṭha, Āṣāḍha, Śrāvaṇa, Bhādra, Āśvina, Kārtika, Agrahāyaṇa, Pauṣa, Māgha, Phālguna, Caitra, but the precessional sequence is in the opposite order. Before Caitra, Vaiśākha would have represented this beginning. Thus the Mahābhārata appears to remember a tradition that was earlier than that of the Śatapatha.

Recent estimates of the date of the Śatapatha Brāhmaṇa, using new hydrological evidence,[24]are relevant to this discussion. Briefly, it is now believed that the Sarasvatī river dried up around 1900 BC due to a massive earthquake that caused its tributary Yamunā to be captured by the Gaṅgā. Since the

Ṛgveda lauds the Sarasvatī as the great river that flows from the mountain to the sea, this Veda should be prior to the date of 1900 BC. According to other authorities, the river stopped flowing all the way to the sea a thousand years earlier, which is why the Harappan sites are not found all the way down to the sea, and 1900 BC represents a further desiccation which led to a collapse of the Harappan economy.

The Śatapatha mentions the disappearance of the Sarasvatī in the desert, and as a text that is not too far separated in time from the Ṛgveda, it should be not be too much later than this catastrophic event.

The astronomical references in the Śatapatha about the Kṛttikās never swerving from the east and the Saptarṣis rising from the north correspond to this general time period. In a new study, Achar[25] argues that these observations indicate around 3000 BC. The Śatapatha itself recorded old tradition, so its own compositional date could be several centuries later.

Earth's precession makes the seasons shift by a nakṣatra every thousand years. If Aśvinī corresponds to about 200 BC, as we know from texts certified to be from that period, Bharaṇī would correspond to 1200 BC. The epochs for the first five nakṣatras will be:

Aśvinī	200 BC
Bharaṇī	1200 BC
Kṛttikā	2200 BC
Rohiṇī	3200 BC
Mṛgaśiras	4200 BC

The lists in the Brāhmaṇas begin with the Kṛttikās indicates that it was drawn up in the third millennium BC. The legend of the cutting off of Prajāpati's head indicates a time when the year began with Mṛgaśīrṣa in the fifth millennium BC. Scholars have also argued that a subsequent list began with Rohiṇī. This argumentation is supported by the fact that there are two Rohiṇīs, separated by fourteen nakṣatras, indicating that the two marked the beginning of the two half-years.

The Śatapatha Brāhmaṇa story of the marriage between the Seven Sages, the stars of the Ursa Major, and the Kṛttikās is elaborated in the Purāṇas where it is stated that the ṛṣis remain for a hundred years in each nakṣatra. In other words, during the earliest times in India there existed a centennial calendar with a cycle of 2,700 years. Called the Saptarṣi calendar, it is still in use in several parts of India. Its current beginning is taken to be 3076 BC, but the notices by the Greek historians Pliny and Arrian suggest that, during the Mauryan times, this calendar was taken to begin in 6676 BC. All this indicates that there was a very ancient tradition of calendrics in India and therefore a memory of the seasons beginning with Caitra is not surprising.

The holding of the Aśvamedha in Caitra points to this rite having been celebrated in the 3rd or the 4th millennium BC. This accords with the traditional date associated with the Mahābhārata War. This accords with the fact that the Mahābhārata contains very ancient material which was revised and enlarged repeatedly right into the classical times.

Royal Power

The statement of Śatapatha 13.1.6.3, *rāṣṭram vā aśvamedhaḥ*, the Aśvamedha means the national (or royal) sway, sums up the various aspects of the sacrifice very well. It associates all classes of people in its year-long ritual. The soldiers protecting the sacrificial horse come from different classes too. The ritual emphasizes dichotomies of class and power, and the sacrifice shows a way to transcend these in the sacred enactment.

The power of the king, mirroring the power of Brahman in the cave of the heart, arises out of its location. Like the "Sun in the rock", a phrase used for the Ātman or Brahman in the Ṛgveda (RV 1.130.3), it is hidden and transcendent. The brahma- and the kṣatra-powers are structurally similar.

The Ṛgveda tells us that power is, at its deepest level, embodiment of the observation process:

dvā suparṇā sayujā sakhāyā

samānṃ vṛkṣam pari ṣasvajāte
tayor anyaḥ pipplalṃ svādv atty
anaṣnann anyo abhi cākaśīti

> Two birds, friends joined together, clutch the same tree. One of them eats the sweet fruti; the other looks on without eating. (RV 1.164.20)

This idea is expressed similarly in the Sāṃkhyan system, where the puruṣa provides the observational counterfoil to the incessant activity of the prakṛti. The king, like this puruṣa, is in the background, whereas the prakṛti represented by the queens, soldiers, priests, and the public is centerstage.

The theme of a four-fold division of royal power runs throughout the rite. The four divisions are the cardinal directions; they are also the base, the body, the activity, and the vision of the king and their embodiment. The reference to the four divisions is to emphasize the gathering together of the Universe that is broken into so many parts in ordinary appearance.

The power of the king rises to the heaven as the Sun ascends the heaven after its rejuvenation.

Renewal of the Cosmic Order

The theme of the preservation of the cosmic order in face of change is to be seen in hymns such as RV 1.24 and 5.2 where there is mention of the freeing of Śunaḥśepa, "Dog's organ," who appears to be the star Kochab in Ursa Minor. This alludes to the stars shifting from their original location due to the precession of the Earth. The identification of Śunaḥśepa becomes clear when you note that his brothers are named Śunaḥpuccha and Śunolāṅgūla (AB 7.14), who are the "Dog tail" Polaris and Pherked. The hero of this cosmic drama is Śunaḥśepa because he, unlike his brothers, deviates the least from the original location in the sky. The Śunaḥśepa story is given a prominent place in the Rājasūya ceremonies.

There is a three-fold drama of change and renewal suggested here. First, is the cosmic layer related to preservation in spite of precession and the stars losing their bearings. Second, is the strengthening of the Sun in the spring after the weakening in the winter. Third, is the mirroring of these processes in the spirit of the Sacrificer. The king, by virtue of his authority and responsibility, sees the dangers to his position magnified many times over those faced by a commoner.

Mythologies from across the world code the drama of the gradual displacement of the constellations marking veral and autumnal equinox and summer and winter solstice by new constellations to the west of them. In Greek mythology, for example, Phaethon's loss of control of the solar chariot represents the end of the golden age; the kicking by Zeus of Lykaon's dish marks the end of the silver age when Taurus and Scorpio had replaced Gemini and Sagittarius as the constellations governing the equinoxes.[26]

The renewal of the Sun represents, symbolically, the other renewals at the cosmic and spiritual levels and in the authority of the king.

It is not surprising that the rebirth of the Sun lies at the basis of ritual in other societies as well. The idea of the sacrifice of the Sun-symbol became the basis of the central practice of Christianity. Scholars are agreed that much of its mythology was taken from the Mithraic religion of the Sun, in which the celebration of the rebirth of the Sun (quite like that of the Aśva as the Sun) was a central feature. According to Cumont,[27] the details of the Christian ritual bear this out:

> Perhaps the custom of invoking the Sun three times each day,—at dawn, at noon, and at dusk,—was reproduced in the daily prayers of the Church, and it appears certain that the commemoration of the Nativity was set for the 25th of December, because it was at the winter solstice that the rebirth of the invincible god, the *Natalis invicti*, was celebrated.

Even now, the Catholic ritual recreates the sacrifice of

Christ and drinking of his blood. Nevertheless, such ritual is basically different from Vedic ritual since it does not admit the possibility of transcendence.

The deep cosmic basis of the Aśvamedha rite makes it certain that it could not have evolved out of a sacrifice that originally involved the killing of a horse. The horse merely serves to symbolize the Sun and we have shown evidence from within the texts that this representation was done by a variety of icons.

If one were to look at the evolutionary process from the secular world in Rome, we find that it was later that dramatic performances were superseded by violent spectacles involving the death of humans and beasts. Given the deep mystical foundation of Vedic ritual, it is certain that it had the inner sacrifice as its prototype.

Even in the case of the Ajamedha (the goat sacrifice), the original symbolic meaning was the sacrifice of the "unborn" (Aja, who stands for the puruṣa) and the actual killing of the goat, wherever it was not substituted by the "killing" of grain (as argued by later texts), primarily served the useful function of the feeding of the participants.

A Universal Rite

The Sun referred to in the Vedas is as often the Sun of the inner firmament as that of the outer sky. The Aśvamedha, while celebrating the beginning of the Year also celebrates the renewal of one's being.

Let's have the Śatapatha 3.5.3) speak on this directly:

> The sacrifice is man. The Soma-cart (shed) is no other than his head, and has Viṣṇu for its deity. And because Soma is therein — Soma being havis (material for offering) for the gods — therefore it is called Havirdhāna (receptacle of havis).
>
> The Āhavanīya is no other than his mouth: hence, when he offers on the Āhavanīya, it is as if he poured (food) into the mouth.

> The sacrificial stake is no other than his crestlock; and the Āgnīdhrīya and Mārjālīya are his arms.
>
> The Sadas (the tent for the priests) is no other than his belly.
>
> And the two fires which are behind it are his feet.

The devas (gods) are the projections of the Brahman within the Sacrificer and the participants. The Śatapatha 3.2.2.14 says, "The vital airs are born of the mind, endowed with the mind, of intelligent power: Agni is speech, Mitra and Varuṇa are the out-breathing and the in-breathing, Āditya (the Sun) is the eye, and the Viśve-Devaḥ are the ear — it is unto these deities that offering is made."

Several pentatonic and hexatonic series of notes (tānas) of music were named after Vedic rites.[28] For example, *ni-dha-pa-ma-ga-ri* was called Agniṣṭoma, *ri-ni-dha-pa-ma-ga* was known as Aśvamedha, and *ma-ga-sa-ni-dha-pa* was called Mahāvrata. This musical aspect of the rites needs further investigation.

The domestic animals of the Aśvamedha represent the physical centers, the wild animals represent the cognitive centers. The horse is the imagined self that must be transformed in resonance with the rhythms of Ṛta. The annual transformation proceeds in step with the transformation of the Sun. The physical centers are renewed by connecting them to the spirit.

The animals are real or icons or they may be the various movements of the Sāman. They are also the stars in the firmament of the Inner and the Outer skies. The Aśvamedha operates at various levels. The full ritual may be viewed as a simultaneous enactment of the various levels, or it may be represented in its essence by the simplest iconic or verbal description.

It appears that the prototype of this rite required just a few days and it was relatively simple. The pageantry of the 101 horses, and hundreds of soldiers and attendants, arose in an embellished version prescribed for kings.

Even now the householder ritual is declared to be thousands of times superior to the Aśvamedha which comparison preserves, no doubt, a memory of the times when it was performed more widely.

Abbreviations

AB	Aitareya Brāhmaṇa
AV	Atharvaveda
BU	Bṛhadāraṇyaka Upaniṣad
IU	Īśāvāsya Upaniṣad
CU	Chāndogya Upaniṣad
GB	Gopatha Brāhmaṇa
KeU	Kena Upaniṣad
KU	Kaṭha Upaniṣad
Mb	Mahābhārata
PB	Pañcaviṃśa Brāhmaṇa
RV	Ṛgveda
ŚB	Śatapatha Brāhmaṇa (Mādhyandina)
TS	Yajurveda–Taittirīya Saṃhitā
VS	Yajurveda–Vājasaneyi Saṃhitā

Notes

1. See the introductory essay by Eggeling (1988); see also the introductions by Keith (1961, 1971). Their early ideas, like those of Oldenberg who considered Soma sacrifice as a rain spell, have been superseded by recent scholarship. For a more interesting review of Vedic sacrifice, see Heesterman (1957) who examines the Rājasūya in considerable depth. But I am not persuaded by Heesterman's thesis (1993) that reflection and abstraction ultimately ended the logic of sacrifice. For general background to the Śrauta ritual, see Dandekar (1958).

2. See Eggeling (1988), Staal (1983), and Tripāṭhī (1990) for a detailed account of the Agnicayana ritual; Kak (2000a,b) presents the astronomy behind these rites.

3. Anthony et al (1991).

4. Smith (1987).

5. Girard (1979), Burkert (1987).

6. Heesterman (1993).

7. Heesterman (1993), page 215.

8. De Nicolas (1976).

9. Kak (2001b).

10. See Kak (2001a) for a review of this material.

11. Gupt (1995), (2001).

12. Napier (1986); see also Napier (2001).

13. Gupt (2001).

14. See Ganguli (1970) for a translation of the relevant sections; Vol. 12, pages 131, 141, 152-3, 163-7.

15. The new year in the pūrṇimānta system is taken to begin in the middle of Caitra (Chatterjee and Chakravarty, 1985).

16. De Santillana and von Dechend (1969) say this about animal stories and mythology as they relate to cosmology, "Today's children, that impassive posterity to whom all reverence is due, know where to look for myths: in the *Jungle Books,* in the stories of Lassie and Flipper, where innocence is unassailable, in Western adventures suitably arranged by grownups for the protection of law and order... The assumed curious child would have been pleased only if he had been told the "story" of the engine just as Kipling tells it, which is hardly the style of a mechanical engineer. But suppose now the child had been confronted with the "story" of a planet as it emerges from the textbooks of celestial mechanics, and had been asked to calculate its orbits and perturbations. This would be a task for a joyless grownup, and a professional one at that. Who else could face the pages bristling with partial differential equations, with long series of approximations, with integrals contrived from pointless quadratures? Truly a world of reserved knowledge. But if, on the other hand, a person living several thousand years ago had been confronted with cunningly built tales of Saturn's reign, and of his exorbitant building and modeling activities—after he had "separated Heaven and Earth" by means of that fateful sickle, that is, after he had established the obliquity of the ecliptic... If he had heard of Jupiter's ways of command and his innumerable escapades, populating the earth with gently nymphs forever crossed in their quest for happiness, escapades that were invariably successful in spite of the constant watchfulness of his jealous "ox-eyed" or sometimes "dog-eyed" spouse... If this person also learned of the fierce adventures of Mars, and the complex mutual involvement of gods and heroes expressing themselves in terms of actions and unvarying numbers, he would have been a participant in the process of mythical knowledge." [page 52-53]

    De Santillana and von Dechend are not aware of the bandhu between the outer and the inner, however.

17. De Santillana and von Dechend (1969), page 53. Also see Zimmer (1946) for a background on Vedic mythology.

18. Heesterman (1957), page 224.

19. De Santillana and von Dechend (1969) discuss at length the centrality of the motion of Sirius in many ancient mythologies.

20. Sankarananda (1944) argues that Aśvaka in VS 23.18 stands for small Aśva, a small fire. He adds, "After spending the whole night in vigil near the fire, the wife of the sacrificer, with her husband, prays to the Sun at day-break in these words: 'Ye the lord of man, ye the dearest of dears, ye the lord of riches, I do invoke thee, my saviour. Ah, the concealer of the Sun within her womb, the night, is born. Ye night you are surely born.'" Also see Vedālaṅkāra (1991).

21. Bodewitz (1990), page 11. Likewise, in the Pravargya ritual the participants wish to acquire the lustre of the Sun (Houben, 1991).

22. Heesterman (1985).

23. Bodewitz (1990).

24. Kak (2000).

25. Achar (2000); see Sastry (1985) for background on Vedic astronomy and the nakṣatras.

26. De Santillana and von Dechend (1969) discuss this at length; see also Brecher and Feirtag (1979).

27. Cumont (1956), pages 195-196.

28. See Mataṅga's Bṛhaddeśī. Also see Bharata Muni's Nāṭyaśāstra (Ghosh, 1967).

References

B.N.N. Achar, "On the astronomical basis of the date of Śatapatha Brāhmaṇa." *Indian Journal of History of Science*, vol. 35, 2000, pp. 1-19.

D. Anthony, D.Y. Telegin, and D. Brown,"The origin of horseback riding." *Scientific American*, December 1991, pp. 94-100.

H.W. Bodewitz, *The Jyotiṣṭoma Ritual.* E.J. Brill, Leiden, 1990.

K. Brecher and M. Feirtag (eds.), *Astronomy of the Ancients.* The MIT Press, Cambridge, 1979.

W. Burkert, *Homo Necans: The Anthropology of Ancient Greek Sacrificial Ritual and Myth.* University of California Press, Berkeley, 1987.

S.K. Chatterjee and A.K. Chakravarty, "Indian calendar from post-Vedic to 1900." *Indian Journal of History of Science*, vol. 20, 1985, pp. 252-307.

F. Cumont, *The Mysteries of Mithra.* Dover, New York, 1956.

R.N. Dandekar (ed.), *Śrautakośa.* Vaidika Saṃśodhana Maṇḍala, Poona, 1958.

A.T. de Nicolas, *Meditations Through the Ṛgveda.* Nicolas-Hayes, York Beach, 1976.

G. de Santillana and H von Dechend, *Hamlet's Mill: An Essay on Myth and the Frame of Time.* Gambit, Boston, 1969.

J. Eggeling (tr.), *The Śatapatha Brāhmaṇa.* Motilal Banarsidass, Delhi, 1988.

K.M. Ganguli (tr.), *The Mahabharata.* Munshiram Manoharlal, New Delhi, 1970.

M. Ghosh (ed. and tr.), *The Nāṭyaśāstra.* Manisha Granthalaya, Calcutta, 1967.

R. Girard, *Violence and the Sacred.* Johns Hopkins Univ Press, Baltimore, 1979.

B. Gupt, *Dramatic Concepts: Greek and Indian.* D.K. Printworld, New Delhi, 1994.

B. Gupt, "From face to interface: journey of *prosopon* and *mukha-rāga* to virtual reality." In *Rūpa Pratirūpa: Mind Man and Mask,* S.C. Malik (ed.). Indira Gandhi National Centre for the Arts & Aryan Books International, New Delhi, 2001, pp. 155-160.

J.C. Heesterman, *The Ancient Indian Royal Consecration.* Mouton, 'S-Gravenhage, 1957.

J.C. Heesterman, *The Inner Conflict of Tradition.* University of Chicago Press, Chicago, 1985.

J.C. Heesterman, *The Broken World of Sacrifice.* University of Chicago Press, Chicago, 1993.

J.E.M. Houben, *The Pravargya Brāhmaṇa of the Taittirīya Āraṇyaka.* Motilal Banarsidass, Delhi, 1991.

S. Kak, *The Astronomical Code of the Ṛgveda.* Munshiram Manoharlal, New Delhi, 2000a.

S. Kak, "Birth and early development of Indian astronomy," In *Astronomy Across Cultures: The History of Non-Western Astronomy.* H. Selin (ed.). Kluwer Academic, Boston, 2000b, pp. 303-340.

S. Kak, "Mind, immortality and art." In *Rūpa Pratirūpa: Mind Man and Mask,* S.C. Malik (ed.). Indira Gandhi National Centre for the Arts & Aryan Books International, New Delhi, 2001a, pp. 16-27.

S. Kak, *The Gods Within.* LSU, Baton Rouge, 2001b.

A.B. Keith, *The Veda of the Black Yajus School.* Motilal Banarsidass, Delhi, 1967.

A.B. Keith, *Rigveda Brahmanas.* Motilal Banarsidass, Delhi, 1971.

A.D. Napier, *Masks, Transformation, and Paradox.* University of California Press, Berkeley, 1986.

A.D. Napier, "Masks and metaphysics in the ancient world: an anthropological view." In *Rūpa Pratirūpa: Mind Man and Mask,* S.C. Malik (ed.). Indira Gandhi National Centre for the Arts & Aryan Books International, New Delhi, 2001, pp. 3-15.

S. Sankarananda, *The Ṛgvedic Culture of the Pre-Historic Indus.* Ramakrishna Vedanta Math, Calcutta, 1944.

T.S.K. Sastry, *Vedāṅga Jyotiṣa of Lagadha.* Indian National Science Academy, New Delhi, 1985.

J.Z. Smith, "The domestication of sacrifice." In *Violent Origins*, R.G. Hamerton (ed.). Stanford University Press, Stanford, 1987.

F. Staal, *Agni. The Vedic Ritual of the Fire Altar.* Asian Humanities Press, Berkeley, 1983.

V. Tripāṭhī, *Agnicayana.* Sampurnananda Sanskrit University, Varanasi, 1990.

R. Vedālaṅkāra, *Ārṣa Jyoti.* Samarpaṇa Śodha Saṃsthāna, Sāhibābād, 1991.

V. Vidyālaṅkāra, *Śatapatha Brāhmaṇastha Agnicayana Samīkṣā.* Dharmartha Trust, Karnal, 1985.

H. Zimmer, *Myths and Symbols in Indian Art and Civilization.* Princeton University Press, Princeton, 1946.

Index